Why Do Cats Meow?

by JOAN HOLUB

illustrations by Anna DiVito

PUFFIN BOOKS

PUFFIN BOOKS
Published by the Penguin Group
Penguin Putnam Books for Young Readers, 345 Hudson Street, New York, New York 10014, U.S.A.
Penguin Books Ltd, 80 Strand, London WC2R ORL, England
Penguin Books Australia Ltd, 250 Camberwell Road, Camberwell, Victoria 3124, Australia
Penguin Books Canada Ltd, 10 Alcorn Avenue, Toronto, Ontario, Canada M4V 3B2
Penguin Books (N.Z.) Ltd, 182-190 Wairau Road, Auckland 10, New Zealand

Penguin Books Ltd, Registered Offices: Harmondsworth, Middlesex, England

First published by Dial Books for Young Readers and Puffin Books,
divisions of Penguin Putnam Books for Young Readers, 2001

15 14 13

Text copyright © Joan Holub, 2001
Illustrations copyright © Anna DiVito, 2001
All rights reserved

THE LIBRARY OF CONGRESS HAS CATALOGED THE DIAL EDITION AS FOLLOWS:
Holub, Joan.
Why do cats meow? / Joan Holub.
p.   cm.
Summary: Questions and answers present information about the history, behavior,
and characteristics of cats and their interaction with humans.
ISBN 0-8037-2503-5 (hardcover)
1. Cats—Behavior—Miscellanea—Juvenile literature. 2. Cats—Miscellanea—Juvenile literature.
[1. Cats—Miscellanea. 2. Questions and answers.] I. Title.
SF446.5.H66 2001 636.8—dc21 00-023985

Puffin Books ISBN 0-14-056788-7
Puffin® and Easy-to-Read® are registered trademarks of Penguin Putnam Inc.

Printed in China

Reading Level 2.3

Photo Credits

Front cover; pages 1, 9, 14, 16, 20, 22, 23 (gray cat and cheetah),
26, 27, 29, 30, 32, 35, 42 copyright © Ron Kimball Studios
Page 8 copyright © Nancy Sheehan
Pages 13, 23 (orange cat), 37, 39 copyright © Davis/Lynn Images

With thanks to Joy and Dena,
my wonderful editors

*Thanks to Stephen Zawistowski, P*H.D.,
*Certified Applied Animal Behaviorist, for his help—*J.H.

*For Ann, Diane, and Justin—*A.D.

Do you love cats?

Many people love cats.

Cats are the most popular pet

in the United States.

Dogs are second.

Cats are good buddies.

Most pet cats are cuddly, playful,

and loving.

How big is the biggest cat?

One pet cat is on record weighing a
whopping forty-seven pounds!
That's as much as a six-year-old child
might weigh.
But most pet cats are much smaller.
They weigh about six
to eighteen pounds.

How much does your cat weigh?

Here is how you can find out:

Weigh yourself.

Hold your cat and weigh yourself again.

Subtract the first number

from the second.

Now you know how much

your cat weighs!

How small is a newborn kitten?

A newborn kitten is so tiny

that it will fit in your hand.

It only weighs about three or four ounces.

When kittens are born, they can't see

or hear.

A kitten's eyes open after a week or so.

It can leave its mother when it is eight
to twelve weeks old.

By the time it is six months old, a kitten
can hunt and take care of itself.

How many kittens can a cat have?

A mother cat usually has two to five kittens at one time.

She could have more than twenty kittens a year.

One cat had four hundred kittens in her lifetime!

Kittens are fun.

But it can be hard to find homes

for so many kittens.

Why do cats meow?

When your cat meows, it could mean

many things.

A soft meow or chirp may be

your cat's way of saying hello.

A loud, long meow means that your cat

wants something.

It may be hungry.

Maybe it wants to play or go outside.

Listen to your cat's different meows.

Try to guess what each one means.

Why do cats purr?

A purr is the soft rumbling sound a cat makes.

Kittens purr when they are nursing.

Cats may purr if they are happy.

Did you know that cats may also purr if they are upset?

Purring makes them feel better.

Pet your cat for a few minutes.

Can you hear it purr?

Why do cats hiss?

Cats hiss when they are mad or afraid.

When a cat hisses, it may also spit,

arch its back, and puff out its fur.

It is trying to look big and scary

to frighten an enemy.

Watch out!

Hissing may mean a cat is ready

to scratch or bite.

Can cats see in the dark?

Cats can see much better than people
can at night.

But they can't see in total darkness.

The back part of a cat's eyes reflects
light like a mirror.

This helps it see with only a tiny bit
of light.

It also makes a cat's eyes glow
in the dark.

In darkness the pupil in the center
of a cat's eye opens wide.

This lets in as much light as possible
to help the cat see better.

Look at your eyes in a mirror.

Do the pupils in your eyes get bigger
in low light too?

Can cats hear sounds that people can't hear?

Does your cat ever act like it hears something—when you don't hear anything?

Cats can hear very high sounds,

such as mouse squeaks,

that people and dogs cannot hear.

A cat's ears turn to listen for

danger sounds.

What is the difference between wild cats and pet cats?

Lions, tigers, and leopards are all wild cats.

Pet cats and wild cats have a lot in common.

They both like to hunt.

They both like to spend time alone.

They both like to play.

But there are many differences too.

Wild cats are usually bigger than pet cats.

They live in jungles and forests.

They do not trust people.

Your cat learned to trust people when it
was a kitten.

Why do pet cats hunt?

Wild cats hunt for food.

But pet cats like to hunt even if they are
fed by people.

Mother cats teach their kittens to hunt
by bringing mice and birds to them.

If your cat brings a mouse or bird

to you, don't get mad.

Your cat is giving you a present

to help you learn to hunt and

to show it loves you.

Just ask your parents to bury your

cat's gift.

Why do cats have claws?

Cats have five toes on each front paw
and four toes on each back paw.
One claw is hidden in each toe.
Cats can slide their claws out when they
need them.
They use their claws to climb, hunt,
or fight.

Why do cats scratch?

Cats sometimes scratch furniture to
sharpen their claws.

They scratch marks on trees to tell
other cats they have been there.

Cats may scratch other animals
if they get scared.

Never pull a cat's tail or play too rough.

The cat won't like it and may
scratch you!

Why do cats have whiskers?

Cat whiskers are thick, stiff hairs.

A cat has about twelve whiskers

on each side of its face.

If it loses a whisker, it can grow a

new one.

Its whiskers grow a little longer than its body is wide.

When a cat pokes its head into a small space, its whiskers tell it if the rest of its body will fit.

Whiskers also help cats find their way in the dark.

Why do cats have tails?

People hold out their arms to keep
their balance when they walk
on a balance beam.
A cat uses its tail in the same way.
It moves its tail back and forth
to help keep its balance.

When a cat holds its tail high,

it is probably happy.

If its tail droops down, it is unhappy

or scared.

If the tip of its tail waves very quickly,

your cat may be ready to pounce!

How much do cats sleep?

Cats sleep about sixteen hours a day.

They are only awake for eight hours!

How many hours do you sleep?

Cats take lots of short naps,

called catnaps.

Does your cat ever twitch while it

is sleeping?

This could mean it is dreaming.

What do you think your cat

dreams about?

Do cats need baths?

Most cats don't like to get wet.
So they won't like it if you give
them a bath.
But cats usually don't need baths.
They lick their fur to get clean.
A cat's tongue feels rough,
like sandpaper.

Try to lick your ear.

You can't, can you?

Cats can't lick their ears either.

They wash their ears by licking

a front paw and rubbing it

behind each ear.

Why does your cat like to rub against you?

Cats do this because it feels good.

They are also rubbing their cat smell

on you.

People can't smell this cat smell—

but other cats can.

Your cat is telling them that it owns you.

So they had better stay away!

Why do cats like to be petted?

Most cats like to be petted because it feels good.

Mother cats lick their kittens to smooth their fur.

When you pet your cat, it reminds your cat of being licked by its mother.

Why do cats go in and out so much?

Your cat thinks it owns your house
and yard.

An indoor cat patrols the rooms
in a house.

It watches cats and birds
through the windows.

An outdoor cat likes to go outside
to see if anything has changed.
It checks to see if other cats have
visited and left their cat smell.
It will also rub against trees and fences
to leave its own cat smell behind.
Then it likes to come back inside
where it is safe and cozy.

Are there any cat heroes?

Scarlett

A mother cat named Scarlett was
very brave.
She lived in an empty building
with her five kittens.
One day the building caught on fire.
Scarlett carried her kittens outside,
one by one.
She risked her life to save her kittens.
There was danger each time she carried
a kitten from the fire.

Zowie

Zowie is a cat that visits people
who are lonely or sick.

Zowie is very brave.

She is not afraid of loud noises or
moving wheelchairs.

Zowie stays calm when strangers
pet her.

When Zowie comes for a visit,
she makes people smile.

What toys do cats like?

Does your cat chase your pencil when you write or draw?

Cats like to play with things that move. They are pretending to hunt, just like wild cats!

Boing! Boing!

A Ping-Pong ball makes a great cat toy.

Draw a picture on one to make

it special.

Use a marker that is child-safe

and will not rub off.

Roll the ball down a long hall

and watch your cat go!

Ssssnake!

Get a long piece of string.

You can tie a ribbon or paper bow

to the end for extra fun.

Wiggle the string snake.

Pull it behind you as you walk.

Watch your cat hunt the snake.

Fishing pole

Tie a string to one end of a stick.

Tie the other end of the string to a small

foam or newspaper ball.

Now go fishing!

Dangle the ball in front of your cat.

Swish it around.

Watch your cat chase the ball.

Kitty condo

Find a large box and ask an adult

to cut different-size holes in it.

Decorate the box so it looks like

a house for your cat.

You can also add cat pictures, your cat's

name, and paw prints.

Watch your cat have fun going in and

out of the holes.

Catnip mouse

Draw a mouse face on the toe
of an old white sock.

Pour a little catnip into the sock.

Tie a knot in the top of the sock.

Let your cat sniff it.

Some cats act silly when they
smell catnip.

Does yours?

Cats may act like they can take care of themselves.

But cats need people to help take care of them.

Your cat loves you and needs you . . . and it wants you to love it back.